The Key Facts™ on

Laos

Essential Information on Laos

By Patrick W. Nee

The Internationalist®

www.internationalist.com

The Internationalist®

International Business, Investment, and Travel

Published by:

The Internationalist Publishing Company

96 Walter Street/ Suite 200

Boston, MA 02131, USA

Tel: 617-354-7722

www.internationalist.com

PN@internationalist.com

Table Of Contents

Chapter 1: Background

Modern-day Laos has its roots in the ancient Lao kingdom of Lan Xang, established in the 14th century under King FA NGUM. For 300 years Lan Xang had influence reaching into present-day Cambodia and Thailand, as well as over all of what is now Laos. After centuries of gradual decline, Laos came under the domination of Siam (Thailand) from the late 18th century until the late 19th century when it became part of French Indochina. The Franco-Siamese Treaty of 1907 defined the current Lao border with Thailand. In 1975, the communist Pathet Lao took control of the government ending a six-century-old monarchy and instituting a strict socialist regime closely aligned to Vietnam. A gradual, limited return to private enterprise and the liberalization of foreign investment laws began in 1988. Laos became a member of ASEAN in 1997 and the WTO in 2013.

Chapter 2: Geography

Location:

Southeastern Asia, northeast of Thailand, west of Vietnam

Geographic coordinates:

18 00 N, 105 00 E

Map references:

Southeast Asia

Area:

total: 236,800 sq km

country comparison to the world: 84

land: 230,800 sq km

water: 6,000 sq km

Area - comparative:

slightly larger than Utah

Land boundaries:

total: 5,083 km

border countries: Burma 235 km, Cambodia 541 km,

China 423 km, Thailand 1,754 km, Vietnam 2,130 km

Coastline:

0 km (landlocked)

Maritime claims:

none (landlocked)

Climate:

tropical monsoon; rainy season (May to November); dry

season (December to April)

Terrain:

mostly rugged mountains; some plains and plateaus

Elevation extremes:

lowest point: Mekong River 70 m

highest point: Phu Bia 2,817 m

Natural resources:

timber, hydropower, gypsum, tin, gold, gemstones

Land use:

arable land: 5.91%

permanent crops: 0.42%

other: 93.67% (2011)

Irrigated land:

3,100 sq km (2005)

Total renewable water resources:

333.5 cu km (2011)

Freshwater withdrawal (domestic/industrial/agricultural):

total: 3.49 cu km/yr (4%/5%/91%)

per capita: 588.9 cu m/yr (2005)

Natural hazards:

floods, droughts

Environment - current issues:

unexploded ordnance; deforestation; soil erosion; most of
the population does not have access to potable water

Environment - international agreements:

party to: Biodiversity, Climate Change, Climate Change-Kyoto Protocol, Desertification, Endangered Species, Environmental Modification, Law of the Sea, Ozone Layer Protection

signed, but not ratified: none of the selected agreements

Geography - note:

landlocked; most of the country is mountainous and thickly forested; the Mekong River forms a large part of the western boundary with Thailand

Chapter 3: People and Society

Nationality:

> noun: Lao(s) or Laotian(s)
>
> adjective: Lao or Laotian

Ethnic groups:

> Lao 55%, Khmou 11%, Hmong 8%, other (over 100 minor ethnic groups) 26% (2005 census)

Languages:

> Lao (official), French, English, various ethnic languages

Religions:

> Buddhist 67%, Christian 1.5%, other and unspecified 31.5% (2005 census)

Population:

> 6,803,699 (July 2014 est.)
>
> country comparison to the world: 104

Age structure:

> 0-14 years: 34.8% (male 1,195,364/female 1,173,520)
>
> 15-24 years: 21.3% (male 719,205/female 728,729)
>
> 25-54 years: 35% (male 1,176,018/female 1,208,452)
>
> 55-64 years: 3.8% (male 169,291/female 175,815)
>
> 65 years and over: 3.7% (male 116,299/female 141,006)
>
> (2014 est.)

Dependency ratios:

> total dependency ratio: 63.8 %

> youth dependency ratio: 57.6 %

> elderly dependency ratio: 6.2 %

> potential support ratio: 16.1 (2013)

Median age:

> total: 22 years

> male: 21.7 years

> female: 22.3 years (2014 est.)

Population growth rate:

> 1.59% (2014 est.)

> country comparison to the world: 78

Birth rate:

> 24.76 births/1,000 population (2014 est.)

> country comparison to the world: 58

Death rate:

> 7.74 deaths/1,000 population (2014 est.)

> country comparison to the world: 110

Net migration rate:

> -1.1 migrant(s)/1,000 population (2014 est.)

> country comparison to the world: 150

Urbanization:

> urban population: 34.3% of total population (2011)

> rate of urbanization: 4.41% annual rate of change (2010-15 est.)

Major urban areas - population:

VIENTIANE (capital) 799,000 (2009)

Sex ratio:

at birth: 1.04 male(s)/female

0-14 years: 1.02 male(s)/female

15-24 years: 0.99 male(s)/female

25-54 years: 0.97 male(s)/female

55-64 years: 0.99 male(s)/female

65 years and over: 0.82 male(s)/female

total population: 0.99 male(s)/female (2014 est.)

Maternal mortality rate:

470 deaths/100,000 live births (2010)

country comparison to the world: 21

Infant mortality rate:

total: 54.53 deaths/1,000 live births

country comparison to the world: 33

male: 60.19 deaths/1,000 live births

female: 48.64 deaths/1,000 live births (2014 est.)

Life expectancy at birth:

total population: 63.51 years

country comparison to the world: 182

male: 61.54 years

female: 65.56 years (2014 est.)

Total fertility rate:

2.9 children born/woman (2014 est.)

country comparison to the world: 60

Contraceptive prevalence rate:

38.4% (2005)

Health expenditures:

2.8% of GDP (2011)

country comparison to the world: 180

Physicians density:

0.19 physicians/1,000 population (2009)

Hospital bed density:

0.7 beds/1,000 population (2010)

Drinking water source:

improved:

urban: 82.8% of population

rural: 62.7% of population

total: 69.6% of population

unimproved:

urban: 17.2% of population

rural: 37.3% of population

total: 30.4% of population (2011 est.)

Sanitation facility access:

improved:

urban: 87.5% of population

rural: 48% of population

total: 61.5% of population

<u>unimproved</u>:

> *urban*: 12.5% of population
>
> *rural*: 52% of population
>
> *total*: 38.5% of population (2011 est.)

HIV/AIDS - adult prevalence rate:

> 0.3% (2012 est.)
>
> <u>country comparison to the world</u>: 96

HIV/AIDS - people living with HIV/AIDS:

> 11,500 (2012 est.)
>
> <u>country comparison to the world</u>: 99

HIV/AIDS - deaths:

> 400 (2012 est.)
>
> <u>country comparison to the world</u>: 98

Major infectious diseases:

> <u>degree of risk</u>: very high
>
> <u>food or waterborne diseases</u>: bacterial and protozoal diarrhea, hepatitis A, and typhoid fever
>
> <u>vectorborne diseases</u>: dengue fever and malaria
>
> <u>note</u>: highly pathogenic H5N1 avian influenza has been identified in this country; it poses a negligible risk with extremely rare cases possible among US citizens who have close contact with birds (2013

Obesity - adult prevalence rate:

> 2.6% (2008)
>
> <u>country comparison to the world</u>: 179

Children under the age of 5 underweight:

    31.6% (2006)

    country comparison to the world: 13

Education expenditures:

    2.8% of GDP (2010)

    country comparison to the world: 147

Literacy:

    definition: age 15 and over can read and write

    total population: 72.7%

    male: 82.5%

    female: 63.2% (2005 est.)

School life expectancy (primary to tertiary education):

    total: 10 years

    male: 11 years

    female: 10 years (2012)

Child labor – children ages 5-14:

    total number: 175,138

    percentage: 11 % (2006 est.)

Chapter 4: Government and Key Leaders

Country name:

> conventional long form: Lao People's Democratic Republic
>
> conventional short form: Laos
>
> local long form: Sathalanalat Paxathipatai Paxaxon Lao
>
> local short form: Pathet Lao (unofficial)

Government type:

> Communist state

Capital:

> name: Vientiane (Viangchan)
>
> geographic coordinates: 17 58 N, 102 36 E
>
> time difference: UTC+7 (12 hours ahead of Washington, DC during Standard Time)

Administrative divisions:

> 16 provinces (khoueng, singular and plural) and 1 capital city* (nakhon luang, singular and plural); Attapu, Bokeo, Bolikhamxai, Champasak, Houaphan, Khammouan, Louangnamtha, Louangphabang, Oudomxai, Phongsali, Salavan, Savannakhet, Viangchan (Vientiane)*, Viangchan, Xaignabouli, Xekong, Xiangkhouang

Independence:

> 19 July 1949 (from France)

National holiday:

> Republic Day, 2 December (1975)

Constitution:

previous 1947 (preindependence); latest promulgated 13-15 August 1991; amended 2003 (2003)

Legal system:

civil law system similar in form to the French system

International law organization participation:

has not submitted an ICJ jurisdiction declaration; non-party state to the ICCt

Suffrage:

18 years of age; universal

Executive branch:

chief of state: President Lt. Gen. CHOUMMALI Saignason (since 8 June 2006); Vice President BOUN-GNANG Volachit (since 8 June 2006)

head of government: Prime Minister THONGSING Thammavong (since 24 December 2010); First Deputy Prime Minister Maj. Gen. ASANG Laoli (since May 2002), Deputy Prime Ministers Maj. Gen. DOUANGCHAI Phichit (since 8 June 2006), SOMSAVAT Lengsavat (since 26 February 1998), and THONGLOUN Sisoulit (since 27 March 2001)

cabinet: Ministers appointed by president, approved by National Assembly

elections: president and vice president elected by National Assembly for five-year terms; election last held on 30 April 2011 (next to be held in 2016); prime minister nominated by the president and elected by the National Assembly for five-year term

election results: CHOUMMALI Saignason elected president; BOUN-GNANG Volachit elected vice president; percent of National Assembly vote - NA; THONGSING Thammavong elected prime minister; percent of National Assembly vote - NA

Legislative branch:

unicameral National Assembly (132 seats; members elected by popular vote from a list of candidates selected by the Lao People's Revolutionary Party to serve five-year terms)

elections: last held on 30 April 2011 (next to be held in 2016)

election results: percent of vote by party - NA; seats by party - LPRP 128, independents 4

Judicial branch:

Highest court(s): People's Supreme Court (consists of NA judges)

judge selection and term of office: president of People's Supreme Court elected by National Assembly on recommendation of National Assembly Standing Committee; vice president of People's Supreme Court and judges appointed by National Assembly Standing Committee; term of office NA

> subordinate courts: provincial, municipal, district, and military courts

Political parties and leaders:

> Lao People's Revolutionary Party or LPRP [CHOUMMALI Saignason]; other parties proscribed

Political pressure groups and leaders:

> NA

International organization participation:

> ADB, ARF, ASEAN, CP, EAS, FAO, G-77, IAEA, IBRD, ICAO, ICRM, IDA, IFAD, IFC, IFRCS, ILO, IMF, Interpol, IOC, IPU, ISO (subscriber), ITU, MIGA, NAM, OIF, OPCW, PCA, UN, UNCTAD, UNESCO, UNIDO, UNWTO, UPU, WCO, WFTU (NGOs), WHO, WIPO, WMO, WTO

Diplomatic representation in the US:

> chief of mission: Ambassador SENG Soukhathivong (since 4 June 2010)
>
> chancery: 2222 S Street NW, Washington, DC 20008
>
> telephone: [1] (202) 332-6416
>
> FAX: [1] (202) 332-4923

Diplomatic representation from the US:

chief of mission: Ambassador David A. CLUNE (since 16 September 2013)

embassy: 19 Rue Bartholonie, That Dam, Vientiane

mailing address: American Embassy Vientiane, APO AP 96546

telephone: [856] 21-26-7000

FAX: [856] 21-26-7190

Key Leaders:

Pres.	CHOUMMALI Saignason, *Lt. Gen.*
Vice Pres.	BOUN-GNANG Volachit
Prime Min.	THONGSING Thammavong
First Dep. Prime Min.	ASANG Laoli, *Maj. Gen.*
Dep. Prime Min.	DOUANGCHAY Phichit, *Maj. Gen.*
Dep. Prime Min.	SOMSAVAT Lengsavat
Dep. Prime Min.	THONGLOUN Sisoulit
Min. of Agriculture & Forestry	VILAYVANH Phomkhe
Min. of Communications, Transport, Posts, & Construction	SOMMATH Pholsena
Min. of Education & Sports	PHANKHAM Viphavanh
Min. of Energy & Mining	SOULIVONG Daravong
Min. of Finance	PHOUPHET Khamphounvong
Min. of Foreign Affairs	THONGLOUN Sisoulit
Min. of Industry & Commerce	NAM Viyaketh
Min. of Information, Culture, & Tourism	BOSENGKHAM Vongdara
Min. of Interior	KHAMPANE Philavong

Min. of Justice	CHALEUAN Yapaoher
Min. of Labor & Social Welfare	ONECHANH Thammavong
Min. of National Defense	DOUANGCHAY Phichit, *Maj. Gen.*
Min. of Natural Resources & Environment	NOULIN Sinbandith
Min. of Planning & Investment	SOMDY Douangdy
Min. of Post, Telecommunications, & Communication	HIEM Phommachanh
Min. of Public Health	EKSAVANG Vongvichit, *Dr.*
Min. of Public Security	THONGBANH Sengaphone
Min. of Public Works & Transportation	SOMMATH Pholsena
Min. of Science & Technology	BOVIENGKHAM Vongdara
Min. to the Prime Min.'s Office & Head of Public Admin. & Civil Authority	BOUNPHENG Mounphosay
Min. to the Prime Min.'s Office & Head of Sustainable Development	KHAM-OUANE Bouppha
Min. to the Prime Min.'s Office & Head of Water Resources & Environmental Authority	KHEMPHENG Pholsena
Min. to the Prime Min.'s Office	BOUASY Lovansay
Min. to the Prime Min.'s Office	BOUNHEUANG Duangphachanh
Min. to the Prime Min.'s Office	BOUNTIEM Phitsamay
Min. to the Prime Min.'s Office	DOUANGSAVAD Souphanouvang
Min. to the Prime Min.'s Office	ONNEUA Phommachanh
Min. to the Prime Min.'s Office	SAISENGLI Tengbliachu
Min. & Chmn. of National Mekong Ctte.	KHAMLOUAD Sitlakone
Min. & Chmn. of National Tourism Authority	SOMPHONG Mongkhonvilay
Min. & Head of Cabinet, Pres.'s	SOUBANH Sritthirath

Office

Min. & Head of Govt. Secretariats	CHEUANG Sombounkhanh
Chmn., National Narcotics Control Board	SOUBANH Sritthirath
Chmn., Planning & Investment Ctte.	SINLAVONG Khoutphaytoune
Chmn., State Control Commission	ASANG Laoli, *Maj. Gen.*
Chmn., State Inspection Ctte., & Head, Anticorruption Agency	BOUNTHONG Chitmani
Governor, Bank of Laos	SAMPAO Phaysith
Ambassador to the US	SENG Soukhathivong
Permanent Representative to the UN, New York	SALEUMXAY Kommasith

Flag description:

three horizontal bands of red (top), blue (double width), and red with a large white disk centered in the blue band; the red bands recall the blood shed for liberation; the blue band represents the Mekong River and prosperity; the white disk symbolizes the full moon against the Mekong River, but also signifies the unity of the people under the Lao People's Revolutionary Party, as well as the country's bright future

National symbol(s):

elephant

National anthem:

name: "Pheng Xat Lao" (Hymn of the Lao People)

lyrics/music: SISANA Sisane/THONGDY
Sounthonevichit

note: music adopted 1945, lyrics adopted 1975; the anthem's lyrics were changed following the 1975 Communist revolution that overthrew the monarchy

Chapter 5: Economy

Economy - overview:

The government of Laos, one of the few remaining one-party communist states, began decentralizing control and encouraging private enterprise in 1986. The results, starting from an extremely low base, were striking - growth averaged 6% per year from 1988-2008 except during the short-lived drop caused by the Asian financial crisis that began in 1997. Laos' growth exceeded 7% per year during 2008-13. Despite this high growth rate, Laos remains a country with an underdeveloped infrastructure, particularly in rural areas. It has a basic, but improving, road system, and limited external and internal land-line telecommunications. Electricity is available 75% of the country. Laos' economy is heavily dependent on capital-intensive natural resource exports. The labor force, however, still relies on agriculture, dominated by rice cultivation in lowland areas, which accounts for about 25% of GDP and 75% of total employment. Economic growth has reduced official poverty rates from 46% in 1992 to 26% in 2010. The economy also has benefited from high-profile foreign direct investment in hydropower, copper and gold mining, logging, and construction though some projects in these industries have drawn criticism for their environmental impacts. Laos gained Normal Trade

Relations status with the US in 2004. On the fiscal side, Laos initiated a VAT tax system in 2010. Simplified investment procedures and expanded bank credits for small farmers and small entrepreneurs will improve Laos' economic prospects. The government appears committed to raising the country's profile among investors, opening the country's first stock exchange in 2011 and participating in regional economic cooperation initiatives. Laos was admitted to the WTO in 2012. The World Bank has declared that Laos' goal of graduating from the UN Development Program's list of least-developed countries by 2020 is achievable.

GDP (purchasing power parity):

$20.78 billion (2013 est.)

country comparison to the world: 132

$19.18 billion (2012 est.)

$17.78 billion (2011 est.)

note: data are in 2013 US dollars

GDP (official exchange rate):

$10.1 billion (2013 est.)

GDP - real growth rate:

8.3% (2013 est.)

country comparison to the world: 9

7.9% (2012 est.)

8% (2011 est.)

GDP - per capita (PPP):

$3,100 (2013 est.)

country comparison to the world: 177

$2,900 (2012 est.)

$2,700 (2011 est.))

note: data are in 2013 US dollars

Gross national saving:

27.4% of GDP (2013 est.)

country comparison to the world: 37

26.2% of GDP (2012 est.)

25.2% of GDP (2011 est.)

GDP – composition, by end use:

household consumption: 66.9%

government consumption: 9.8%

investment in fixed capital: 31.7%

investment in inventories: -1.3%

exports of goods and services: 40%

imports of goods and services: -48.4% (2013 est.)

GDP - composition by sector:

agriculture: 24.8%

industry: 32%

services: 37.5% (2013 est.)

Agriculture – products:

sweet potatoes, vegetables, corn, coffee, sugarcane, tobacco, cotton, tea, peanuts, rice; cassava (manioc), water buffalo, pigs, cattle, poultry

Industries:

mining (copper, tin, gold, and gypsum); timber, electric power, agricultural processing, rubber, construction, garments, cement, tourism

Industrial production growth rate:

11% (2013 est.)

country comparison to the world: 12

Labor force:

3.373 million (2013 est.)

country comparison to the world: 100

Labor force - by occupation:

agriculture: 75.1%

industry and services: NA (2010 est.)

Unemployment rate:

2.5% (2009 est.)

country comparison to the world: 19

2.4% (2005 est.)

Population below poverty line:

26% (2010 est.)

Household income or consumption by percentage share:

lowest 10%: 3.3%

highest 10%: 30.3% (2008)

Distribution of family income - Gini index:

36.7 (2008)

country comparison to the world: 83

34.6 (2002)

Budget:

revenues: $2.481 billion

expenditures: $2.642 billion (2013 est.)

Taxes and other revenues:

24.6% of GDP (2013 est.)

country comparison to the world: 135

Budget surplus (+) or deficit (-):

-1.6% of GDP (2013 est.)

country comparison to the world: 73

Public Debt:

46.3% of GDP (2013 est.)

country comparison to the world: 78

49.1% of GDP (2012 est.)

Inflation rate (consumer prices):

6.5% (2013 est.)

country comparison to the world: 181

4.3% (2012 est.)

Central bank discount rate:

4.3% (31 December 2010)

country comparison to the world: 95

4% (31 December 2009)

Commercial bank prime lending rate:

23.2% (31 December 2013 est.)

country comparison to the world: 14

22.3% (31 December 2012 est.)

Stock of narrow money:

$1.389 billion (31 December 2013 est.)

country comparison to the world: 142

$1.154 billion (31 December 2012 est.)

Stock of broad money:

$4.071 billion (31 December 2013 est.)

country comparison to the world: 135

$3.673 billion (31 December 2012 est.)

Stock of domestic credit:

$4.716 billion (31 December 2013 est.)

country comparison to the world: 116

$4.034 billion (31 December 2012 est.)

Current account balance:

-$484.3 million (2013 est.)

country comparison to the world: 98

-$315.5 million (2012 est.)

Exports:

$2.313 billion (2013 est.)

country comparison to the world: 140

$1.984 billion (2012 est.)

Exports - commodities:

wood products, coffee, electricity, tin, copper, gold, cassava

Exports - partners:

Thailand 34%, China 21.5%, Vietnam 12.2% (2012)

Imports:

$3.238 billion (2013 est.)

country comparison to the world: 145

$2.744 billion (2012 est.)

Imports - commodities:

machinery and equipment, vehicles, fuel, consumer goods

Imports - partners:

Thailand 62.1%, China 16.2%, Vietnam 7.3% (2012)

Reserves of foreign exchange and gold:

$845.4 million (31 December 2013 est.)

country comparison to the world: 141

$796.9 million (31 December 2012 est.)

Debt - external:

$6.69 billion (31 December 2013 est.)

country comparison to the world: 112

$6.288 billion (31 December 2012 est.)

Exchange rates:

kips (LAK) per US dollar -

7,875.9 (2013 est.)

8,007.3 (2012 est.)

8,258.8 (2010 est.)

8,516.04 (2009)

8,760.69 (2008)

Chapter 6: Energy

Electricity - production:

    3.629 billion kWh (2010 est.)

    country comparison to the world: 127

Electricity - consumption:

    2.355 billion kWh (2010 est.)

    country comparison to the world: 137

Electricity - exports:

    2.02 billion kWh (2010 est.)

    country comparison to the world: 42

Electricity - imports:

    1 billion kWh (2010 est.)

    country comparison to the world: 64

Electricity - installed generating capacity:

    1.895 million kW (2010 est.)

    country comparison to the world: 105

Electricity - from fossil fuels:

    2.6% of total installed capacity (2010 est.)

    country comparison to the world: 201

Electricity - from nuclear fuels:

    0% of total installed capacity (2010 est.)

    country comparison to the world: 122

Electricity - from hydroelectric plants:

    97.4% of total installed capacity (2010 est.)

    country comparison to the world: 9

Electricity - from other renewable sources:

0% of total installed capacity (2010 est.)

country comparison to the world: 191

Crude oil - production:

0 bbl/day (2012 est.)

country comparison to the world: 185

Crude oil - exports:

0 bbl/day (2010 est.)

country comparison to the world: 140

Crude oil - imports:

0 bbl/day (2010 est.)

country comparison to the world: 206

Crude oil - proved reserves:

0 bbl (1 January 2013 es)

country comparison to the world: 152

Refined petroleum products - production:

0 bbl/day (2010 est.)

country comparison to the world: 161

Refined petroleum products - consumption:

3,391 bbl/day (2011 est.)

country comparison to the world: 177

Refined petroleum products - exports:

0 bbl/day (2010 est.)

country comparison to the world: 190

Refined petroleum products - imports:

3,160 bbl/day (2010 est.)

country comparison to the world: 170

Natural gas - production:

0 cu m (2011 est.)

country comparison to the world: 151

Natural gas - consumption:

0 cu m (2010 est.)

country comparison to the world: 162

Natural gas - exports:

0 cu m (2011 est.)

country comparison to the world: 132

Natural gas - imports:

0 cu m (2011 est.)

country comparison to the world: 86

Natural gas - proved reserves:

0 cu m (1 January 2013 es)

country comparison to the world: 156

Carbon dioxide emissions from consumption of energy:

1.404 million Mt (2011 est.)

country comparison to the world: 159

Chapter 7: Communications

Telephones - main lines in use:

112,000 (2012)

country comparison to the world: 143

Telephones - mobile cellular:

6.492 million (2012)

country comparison to the world: 99

Telephone system:

general assessment: service to general public is improving;

the government relies on a radiotelephone network to

communicate with remote areas

domestic: 4 service providers with mobile cellular usage

growing very rapidly

international: country code - 856; satellite earth station - 1

Intersputnik (Indian Ocean region) and a second to be

developed by China (2012)

Broadcast media:

6 TV stations operating out of Vientiane - 3 government-

operated and the others commercial; 17 provincial stations

operating with nearly all programming relayed via satellite

from the government-operated stations in Vientiane;

Chinese and Vietnamese programming relayed via satellite

from Lao National TV; broadcasts available from stations

in Thailand and Vietnam in border areas; multi-channel

satellite and cable TV systems provide access to a wide

range of foreign stations; state-controlled radio with state-operated Lao National Radio (LNR) broadcasting on 5 frequencies - 1 AM, 1 SW, and 3 FM; LNR's AM and FM programs are relayed via satellite constituting a large part of the programming schedules of the provincial radio stations; Thai radio broadcasts available in border areas and transmissions of multiple international broadcasters are also accessible (2012)

Internet country code:

.la

Internet hosts:

1,532 (2012)

country comparison to the world: 166

Internet users:

300,000 (2009)

country comparison to the world: 130

Chapter 8: Transportation

Airports:

    41 (2013)

    country comparison to the world: 103

Airports - with paved runways:

    total: 8

    2,438 to 3,047 m: 3

    1,524 to 2,437 m: 4

    914 to 1,523 m: 1 (2013)

Airports - with unpaved runways:

    total: 33

    1,524 to 2,437 m: 2

    914 to 1,523 m: 9

    under 914 m: 22 (2013)

Roadways:

    total: 39,568 km

    country comparison to the world: 89

    paved: 530 km

    unpaved: 39,038 km (2007)

Waterways:

    4,600 km (primarily on the Mekong River and its tributaries; 2,900 additional km are intermittently navigable by craft drawing less than 0.5 m) (2012)

    country comparison to the world: 24

Chapter 9: Military

Military branches:

Lao People's Armed Forces (LPAF): Lao People's Army (LPA; includes Riverine Force), Air Force (2011)

Military service age and obligation:

18 years of age for compulsory or voluntary military service; conscript service obligation - minimum 18-months (2012)

Manpower available for military service:

males age 16-49: 1,574,362

females age 16-49: 1,607,856 (2010 est.)

Manpower fit for military service:

males age 16-49: 1,111,629

females age 16-49: 1,190,035 (2010 est.)

Manpower reaching militarily significant age annually:

male: 71,400

female: 73,038 (2010 est.)

Military expenditures:

NA% (2012)

0.23% of GDP (2011)

NA% (2010)

Military – note:

serving one of the world's least developed countries, the Lao People's Armed Forces (LPAF) is small, poorly funded, and ineffectively resourced; its mission focus is border and internal security, primarily in countering ethnic Hmong insurgent groups; together with the Lao People's Revolutionary Party and the government, the Lao People's Army (LPA) is the third pillar of state machinery, and as such is expected to suppress political and civil unrest and similar national emergencies, but the LPA also has upgraded skills to respond to avian influenza outbreaks; there is no perceived external threat to the state and the LPA maintains strong ties with the neighboring Vietnamese military (2008)

Chapter 10: Transnational Issues

Disputes - international:

southeast Asian states have enhanced border surveillance to check the spread of avian flu; talks continue on completion of demarcation with Thailand but disputes remain over islands in the Mekong River; concern among Mekong River Commission members that China's construction of dams on the Mekong River and its tributaries will affect water levels; Cambodia and Vietnam are concerned about Laos' extensive upstream dam construction

Illicit drugs:

estimated opium poppy cultivation in 2008 was 1,900 hectares, about a 73% increase from 2007; estimated potential opium production in 2008 more than tripled to 17 metric tons; unsubstantiated reports of domestic methamphetamine production; growing domestic methamphetamine problem (2007)

Map of Laos

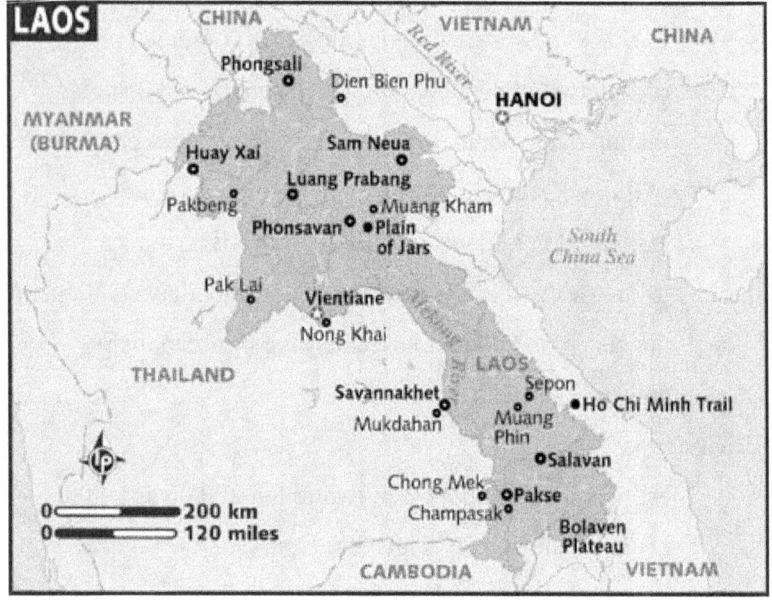

Other Key Facts™ Titles

Key Facts on Syria

Key Facts on China

Key Facts on Qatar

Key Facts on India

Key Facts on Germany

Key Facts on Argentina

Key Facts on Russia

Key Facts on North Korea

Key Facts on Brazil

Key Facts on Italy

Key Facts on the United Arab Emirates

Key Facts on the European Union

Key Facts on Pakistan

Key Facts on Saudi Arabia

Key Facts on Cyprus

Key Facts on Iran

Key Facts on Afghanistan

Key Facts on Iraq

Key Facts on Indonesia

Key Facts on South Korea

Key Facts on France

Key Facts on the United Kingdom

Key Facts on Egypt

Key Facts on Israel

All Key Facts™ Titles are Available at

www.Amazon.com

THE INTERNATIONALIST®

2014

WWW.INTERNATIONALIST.COM

www.ingramcontent.com/pod-product-compliance
Lightning Source LLC
Chambersburg PA
CBHW070720180526
45167CB00004B/1553